Historical mysteries

in Normandy

SERGE VAN DEN BROUCKE

HISTORICAL MYSTERIES IN NORMANDY

© 2023 SERGE VAN DEN BROUCKE

Édition : BoD – Books on Demand, info@bod.fr
Impression : BoD - Books on Demand, In de Tarpen 42,
Norderstedt (Allemagne)
Impression à la demande

Cover illustration : Jane Spaulding / Pixabay

ISBN : 978-2-3224-7154-6
Dépôt légal : Janvier 2023

For all history buffs and travellers

curious to discover what lies beneath the surface.

FOREWORD

As a French journalist and writer specialising in historical research and heritage, living in Normandy and regularly spending a lot of time in Britain for work and pleasure, I have more than once acted as a guide for British and American friends visiting the region. This is what gave me the idea of writing this little book, which is obviously not exhaustive - it would take volumes to tell everything! - but which is simply an invitation to the history-loving reader to come and discover for himself what a fascinating land Normandy is. But precisely, there is no question here of repeating what one can read everywhere! My research has led me to unveil some surprising secrets....

The historical heritage of Normandy is truly exceptional. Didn't Stendhal write, in 1838, that *"Rouen is the Athens of the Gothic genre"*? Everywhere, from the largest cities to the most modest villages, the history of this extraordinary province unfolds like a long, passionate narrative that an enthusiastic storyteller would recite to his companions in the evening, in front of a crackling fire. Founded more than a thousand years ago by a handful of daring and pragmatic Viking adventurers, the Duchy of Normandy has held a special place in the ever-changing chessboard of ancient Europe for centuries.

The fates of Normandy and Britain have been intimately linked since time immemorial. The mighty winds of history have blown across these two lands, for better or for worse, and to be interested in one is to be interested in the other. Here, historical heritage is both the tragedy of Joan of Arc's trial and the laughter of Falstaff, the spectacular stone work of Rouen Cathedral and modest Bede's monastic cell in Jarrow, Napoleon's equestrian statue in Cherbourg and Nelson's *Victory* in Portsmouth. The Hundred Years' War and the Entente Cordiale. Voltaire in London and Oscar Wilde in Dieppe. You see, the Channel was as much a barricade as a link.

The fascinating thing about exploring bygone eras is that it allows us to bring to life this immense gallery of characters, famous or humble, without whom the world we know would not be what it is. To achieve this, one must dare to push open the door, to immerse oneself in the archives and take pleasure in it, to travel beyond the beaten track, to accept the price of patience, and to marvel at everything.

Then you find yourself, suddenly and sometimes by chance, face to face with the mystery of destiny. For your enjoyment, here are some strange, fascinating and sometimes terrifying, but always true examples!

Hrolf / Rollon, the Viking leader who founded Normandy

A NORMAN CHURCH INVADED BY THE LIVING DEAD

In Normandy, popular culture offers a great wealth of extraordinary tales. This one clearly demonstrates the fears and hopes of people in ancient times.

It was a long time ago on the Normandy coast, in the port of Dieppe, in the Pollet district, the fishermen's quarter, simple and very pious people, used to hard work, aware of the harshness of life and always imminent possible death. That night a strong wind arose. At sea, the swell became powerful, rumbling, furious waves crashed on the pier with a great uproar. Then, the sky was torn, and a terrible storm spewed immense lightning on the Norman little town. Slammed in their homes, the inhabitants quickly closed shutters and doors, with a double turn, to protect themselves from the fury of nature and the evil spirits who could still prowl in the alleys when God manifested his anger. The sacristan of Notre-Dame du Pollet, the small church where everyone came to pray, begging the Lord and all his saints to protect the men who had gone to sea, slept soundly, indifferent to the storm that was raging outside. But suddenly, a familiar sound woke him up from his sleep, and he jumped out of bed: the bell. The bell of Notre-Dame, which had begun to ring. In the middle of the night. How was this possible? What was going on? It was strange.

The sacristan believed at first that he had slept too much, and he thought that morning was already approaching and that he was late. Would someone else have been given the task of ringing the bell? It had never been seen before. He dressed hastily, left his house in a hurry, and realized that it was still pitch dark, that it was raining heavily and that the thunder did not stop. He told himself that was not normal, really not normal. He rushed through the narrow alleys to the church, opened the door, and there …

There, in the dimness barely tempered by the flickering light of a few candles, he vaguely distinguished a compact crowd, absorbed in contemplation. Who were all these people? What was going on here? They were indeed saying a Mass. A priest stood at the altar. Little by little, the sacristan's eyes became accustomed to this semi-darkness in which the whole building was immersed, and he was petrified on the spot. All the participants in this strange ceremony were... dead. Yes, the inhabitants of the Pollet, sailors swept away by the waves, crushed on the rocks, killed by cholera, or simply dead of exhaustion after an existence of too painful labor. The sacristan knew almost all of them, he had attended their funeral, he had offered a word of comfort to their widows and orphans crushed with grief and despair. When the time of communion came, the priest tried to lift the host, but he could not. It was heavier than lead, heavier than if all the angels of heaven clung to it to hold it. His face, or what was left of it, tensed with unspeakable pain, his hands twisted, his body trembling. Then he let out a frightful howl, which spread like a torrent of contagion through the whole crowd of ghosts.

Turning to the sacristan still paralyzed by fear at this macabre spectacle, the priest spoke to him in a chilling voice. « *During my lifetime, I had vowed to offer a mass in honor of Our Lady, but I have been inconsistent, and I forgot my promise. You know me, sacristan, you remember me, my ship broke on the rocks near the cliffs on Easter Monday, and I drowned. Now I am coming back to say this Mass myself, but I cannot achieve it, and I am burning hellfires, like all those you see here, who have committed the same fault. I beg you, go tell my son to never, never forget the masses he promises! Go, carry my message!* » A violent light spattered the whole church, and blinded the sacristan who rushed to the door, shouting with all his might, and fled at full speed in the folds of the night.

This fantastic tale is part of the popular tradition of Dieppe, or more exactly, of the Pollet district. The fishermen of this very particular district, which stood for centuries outside the city walls itself, have over time developed a whole set of legendary stories and customs whose originality and diversity are remarkable. Death very often holds a preponderant place there. The small church in question here, where the living dead gathered, is in fact the medieval chapel of Notre-Dame des Grèves. The origin of this very old building probably dates back to the XI$_{th}$ century, and its construction may have been due to a vow made by an English sailor. Today, Notre Dame des Grèves still exists, but don't expect to be able to observe the original building. This was abandoned at the very request of the inhabitants, who wanted to have a much larger place of worship, capable of accommodating the entire population of Pollet. The pretty chapel from the Middle Ages has been demolished. The current building dates from the XIXth century: work began in 1843, and it was the Archbishop of Rouen who came to inaugurate it in 1849. It was still necessary to wait until 1860 for its bell tower to be finally completed. To be completely honest, Dieppe offers heritage enthusiasts many fascinating buildings rich in history, but one cannot really say, on the other hand, that the architecture of <u>this</u> church is particularly inspiring. The whole building is very angular, of a downright austere appearance, with very few decorations. Moreover, at the time of its inauguration, many voices were heard to criticize it. It was called « *a square box without style* », matching the military barracks and the nearby prison !

The Pollet district, in Dieppe, at the end of the XIXth century.

The port of Dieppe today.

THE VICTORIAN MILITARY HERO WHO MYSTERIOUSLY DIED IN NORMANDY

Let's go now to the city of Caen, in Calvados, to a strange place that very few people notice, or even know: the Protestant cemetery. It is located rue du Magasin à Poudre, right next to the university. Dilapidated, overgrown with ivy and weeds, the place is tiny. When you enter it, you have mixed feelings, sometimes paradoxical, depending on the mood or the season, ranging from romantic reverie to a certain oppression. Hidden in a refreshing bouquet of tall trees that provide pleasant shade, wedged between a street where cars roar and modern buildings with impersonal architecture, it keeps its secrets well.

There, a very modest degraded burial, which we only discover by chance, surmounted by a cross broken by vandals, bears the name of Thomas James Young. An Englishman. Thomas James Young. Who is he ? Just a stranger? No, on the contrary, he is a famous military hero of the Victorian era, forgotten today in this square of Norman land …

Born in London in 1827, Thomas James Young enlisted at thirteen as a simple cadet in the Royal Navy and reached the rank of lieutenant on April 11, 1851, at the age of twenty-four. He served during the Crimean War and in other battles. In 1857, he was aboard the ship HMS Shannon, armed with 50 guns, which cruised in the waters of the Indian subcontinent. The terrible Indian Mutiny raged, and marked a decisive turning point in the history of the British Empire. The city of Lucknow - the current capital of Uttar

Pradesh - which was founded in the 18th century, was the capital of the State of Oudh, and its attachment to English India sparked a bloody revolt of great magnitude . Young and his 200 men were ordered to recapture Lucknow, and free the British Residence building. They left the ship and plunged into hostile territories.

On November 16, in this dangerous city in turmoil, where all minds were heated, violent fighting broke out. Supported by the cannon fire of the Royal Artillery, the English advanced. Nearly 2000 mutineers were killed. At four in the afternoon, Young and his group arrived in front of a seemingly impregnable fortified edifice, the Shah Nujeff. The confrontation was more brutal than ever. Young's men fell one after another under heavy insurgent fire. Soon Thomas was left alone, only accompanied by a loyal sailor, William Hall. They were not discouraged, they hold the position at all costs. The two fighters came close to death a hundred times.

Meanwhile, Sergeant John Paton of the 93rd Highlanders found a rift, rushed through it, and knocked the fortress down. The next day, November 17, 1857, the British Residence, which had been valiantly defended from within by Sir James Outram, was liberated.

In 1859, Thomas James Young returned to London. On June 8, as a reward for his unwavering courage, he received the Victoria Cross from the hand of Queen Victoria herself, during a brilliant ceremony at Buckingham Palace. John Paton and William Hall were also honored by the Sovereign. On June 23, Thomas was promoted to the rank of commander. Other adventures followed: appointed commander of the coast guards in Devon, he married Louisa Mary Boyes the following year, then rose again in rank and became captain in 1866, at the age of thirty-nine. Then, strangely, we lose track …

Thomas James Young died on March 20, 1869 in Caen. What was he doing there? No one knows. It is true that in this second part of the 19th century, a large British community lived in Caen, but that does not explain why Young was there, nor why he died so young, at 42 years old. Some said that he had come to Normandy quite simply on vacation, others said that he had fallen ill, and that he was staying in Caen to take care of his health. It seems to be just speculation.

The answer may have been found in the city's archives, which were unfortunately destroyed during the bombings of July 1944. The enigma therefore remains intact today. In March 2009, the Victoria Cross Society, headquartered in Uppingham, in the small English county of Rutland, launched an appeal for funds from its members to give the tomb of the intrepid warrior a minimum of decency. Thus, on March 10, 2010, after approval by the French authorities, a new small stone slab was placed on the old burial place. It is the one that we see today, when we look carefully. But who will really be able to lift the veil on the last moments of Thomas James Young? This historical mystery remains so far unanswered.

If you are travelling in Normandy and passing through Caen, why not pay a little visit to this forgotten Englishman? He feels so lonely ....

The vandalised grave of T.J. Young, in Caen.

WOULD YOU DARE TO FACE ROBERT THE DEVIL ?

In the small town of Moulineaux, on the banks of the river Seine, not far from Rouen, capital of Normandy, there is a discreet historical site, relatively far from the usual tours, and which nevertheless deserves the attention of history buffs. It is a medieval castle. Oh, of course, it is modest, it has nothing to do with Norman buildings as spectacular as the cathedral of Rouen, the two immense abbeys of Caen, or of course the Mont St Michel. In fact, this site is not so remarkable for its architecture as for the incredible legend attached to it. You will soon understand why. This place, perched on a hill, is the castle of Robert the Devil.

This building was founded in the XIth century. Some say it was by the first Dukes of Normandy, others once claimed that the builder was Richard the Lionheart himself. In fact, it seems that it was first mentioned in a text written in 1180. It is also known that King John, the last son of Henry II and Eleanor of'Aquitaine, came here several times, between 1199 and 1204. Then the building was altered more than once, first rebuilt in the 13th century, then transformed between 1397 and 1418: this last date is probably that of its dismantling and destruction, because this castle, which had been occupied by the English and then returned to the King of France Charles the Fith in 1365, could have fallen back into enemy hands, and could have become a stronghold against Rouen. The first modern excavations took place in 1758, carried out by Rondeaux de Setry. Then, during further research in 1855, burials were discovered in the moat. At the very beginning of the 20th century, the architect Lucien Lefort prepared a project to restore the castle, which was really in ruins at the time, and undertook major work to enhance the historic site. After the Second World War, during which the castle was looted and again degraded, other more or less successful attempts at development took place, and then for many years, brambles and weeds invaded the place. It was not until 2007 that the castle was bought by the metropolis of Rouen, and that a gradual rehabilitation could be programmed. So you can see that a lot of gray areas, and approximations, still remain on the history of this medieval building.

But the most curious, ultimately, is its name. The castle of Robert the Devil. Who was this Robert who was given such a terrifying nickname? Ah, this is where things get complicated .... and also get extremely interesting. For a long time, it was believed that Robert the Devil was in fact Robert the

Magnificent, the father of William the Conqueror. Or Robert Courteheuse, the son of William, and grandson of the Magnificent. These assumptions are completely fanciful, even if some still want to believe them, even today. In 1631, the priest of a village called Manneval, Gabriel Du Moulin, had written a General History of Normandy, in which we find this passage which concerns Robert the Magnificent: *"This prince did not deny the piety of his ancestors, was quiet and gentle to his friends, but a lion in the fires of anger, and a real Robert the Devil "*. In reality, this Robert the Devil is a legendary medieval character from the XIIth century, the hero of a long anonymous poem of chivalry, composed in the Norman style in the XIIIth century, and entitled the Roman de Robert le Diable. After some transformations made by singers and jugglers in the XIVth century, it comprises 254 stanzas of 4 monorhymes, and in the XVth century, a prose version has been written. This is the real origin of the whole affair. But, well, finally, what is the story all about? It all begins in fury and darkness.

In the time of King Pippin, father of Charlemagne, there was in this region which was not yet Normandy a great and powerful lord called Aubert. He was married to the sister of the Duke of Burgundy, Inde. Despite all her prayers, she could not have children. So, out of desperation and as a last resort, she secretly turned to the evil powers, and summoned the devil. Thanks to this pact, her wishes were granted, and she finally gave birth to a boy, whom she named Robert. Growing up, he revealed a dreadful, violent, devious, cruel character, always ready to instigate bad blows, to the point that he ended up leading a militia of dangerous thugs who terrorized all the villagers and committed horrendous crimes in the forest of Rouvray before returning to shut himself up in his castle on the hill of Moulineaux. One day, frightened of the horrors that his personality forced him to perpetrate, as if an inner force was devouring him, he questioned his mother, urged her with questions, insisted constantly. Pushed to the limits, she finally confessed to him the terrible secret of his birth: he was born with the help of the devil's breath !

Robert then left his castle to go to Rome, to meet the Pope and beg him to help him. Once there, the Holy Father demanded that Robert go to meet a wise hermit. This man ordered him, by way of penance, to take a vow of silence and to dispute his food with the dogs. Time passed. Robert had become a miserable wanderer, and one day he crossed paths with the Emperor of Rome, who took pity on him and welcomed him. But the city was in turmoil, looters ravaged the houses and molested the inhabitants. So Robert took his knight's armor, for the first time in a long time, and fought the bandits vigorously, until final victory. To thank him for so much bravery, the emperor offered his daughter's hand to the valiant victor. However Robert, full of modesty, refused this offer. He left the palace, went on the dusty roads, and lived until the end of his days in solitude, meditation and prayer.

Of course, this beautiful story, of which there are several variations, has nothing to do with any historical truth. It is a medieval poetic creation whose edifying conclusion, full of moral sense, aims to strike the spirits. Very anchored in the Norman imagination for centuries, the life of Robert the Devil has fascinated generations.

His fate was even the subject of an opera by Giacomo Meyerbeer with a libretto by Eugène Scribe in 1831. Scribe is a forgotten author today, but in the XIXth century he was one of the greatest glories of the French theatre, a member of the Académie française, with more than 420 plays to his credit, and numerous opera librettos. His collaboration with Meyerbeer for the creation of Robert le Diable led to the emergence and development of the

Grand Opéra, a style of operatic performance in which everything had to be spectacular, bordering on the excessive: the music, the sets, the scenic effects, the whole being based on a historical drama. Robert le Diable was an extraordinary success and blew the audience away as the greatest international films can do today. Balzac himself was astounded and described the work as a temple of illusion and miracle.

The libretto written for the occasion takes great liberties with the medieval legend: here, the action takes place in Sicily and Robert has a foster sister, Alice, promised in marriage to an insolent troubadour. After many twists and turns that place the Norman hero torn between Good and Evil, and memorable fantastic episodes (including a diabolical dance performed by damned and exalted nuns that caused a great scandal!) he succumbs to the love of Isabella, daughter of the King of Sicily. Finally, in this version, all's well that ends well for the lord of Moulineaux castle! And today, when you walk around his fortress, who knows if the ghost of a troubadour will not yet sing about his wonderful adventures?

The ruins of the castle of Robert the Devil.

A TEENAGE BOY ON HIS WAY TO THE HORROR OF THE TRENCHES

His name was René, and he was 16 years old. He lived with his parents in rue Jacquart, on the left bank of Rouen, the capital of Normandy. This street still exists, it has nothing really special, it is located between the rue Saint Julien and the rue Louis Blanc, close to the botanical garden. In this beautiful summer of 1914, the war obviously occupied all minds, and it was believed that it would be quick, and short. No one then could imagine the long years of anguish and horror that were to follow. Nor could one know that this appalling conflict would forever upset the whole of European society, and bring the world into a new era.

René was employed in a pharmacy, and the pharmacist was very satisfied with this boy, perfectly punctual, attentive to his work and pleasant company. Everyone found him nice, efficient and sympathetic. But now René could only think of one thing: to join the army, to go to war, to defend Normandy and France, arms in hand, against a fierce enemy. Like most young people of the time, René was carried away by a great wind of patriotism, and a strong sense of duty. To get involved and go and fight to save the nation, it was obvious to him. He then presented himself to the military office, determined to take part in the events, immediately. His enthusiasm was rapidly dampened, for the recruiter informed him that they weren't hiring such young people after all, and sent him home. Willing to carry out his project in spite of everything, René quickly made acquaintances among the English soldiers stationed in Rouen. He was doing them little services, he knew how to make himself appreciated, and of course he told them that he wanted to go fight, by whatever means. While hanging out with the British, he even made the effort to start jabbering a little English, a few words, a few expressions, and that made his new friends laugh.

One night, in a smoky bar, they ended up saying to him, probably just jokingly: If you can't join the French army, why not try the British army? Well, it hadn't fallen on deaf ears. A bit later, one evening, he returned to his parents ... wearing a khaki uniform of His Majesty! In front of their astonished expression, he announced to them that he had managed to be accepted as a soldier by the British army! We do not really know how the case was settled, but anyway it was not really legal, because he had obviously not signed any paper! Still, this time, he was really on his way to an exciting adventure!

On august 10, 1914, René left Rouen, embarked on a ship with the English as far as Saint-Nazaire, then he was sent to Paris and Soissons. At this stage, nobody expected him to go skewer the enemy with the bayonet. During all the weeks that followed, he was entrusted with odd jobs, especially housekeeping duties. He worked first in the kitchens, then in the medical trains, before going up to the north of France and crossing the border to go to Belgium.

At that time, René did not feel very well, a few days passed, and he fell really ill. His condition was perhaps not very serious, we do not really know, but it was worrying enough. The English quickly repatriated him to Boulogne, to be admitted to a French hospital. And there, surprise ! They realized that this boy was not on any list, and was not part of any battalion! And he was refused admission to the hospital! He then had to come back on his own to Rouen for treatment, where his parents, who were very decent people, were still absolutely convinced that their son was really legally engaged, as he had told them.

René arrived at Saint-Sever station. Today, the Rouen railway station is located on the right bank, but in 1914 it was on the left bank: this station was built in 1843, it was inaugurated by the Duke of Nemours. Nowadays, it no longer exists, it was destroyed by the bombardments of 1944, and never rebuilt. René asked an employee for information. It was a very bad idea: the man stared at him, giving him a suspicious look. A young boy all alone in an English uniform but speaking French without the slightest accent, well, it was weird. The employee called for reinforcements. The railway workers abruptly seized the unfortunate teenager, and summoned the police forces who accused René of illegally wearing a uniform in time of war. In other words, court martial. In other words, a conviction without appeal. In other words, a death sentence. René was immediately taken before the Public Prosecutor, to whom he gave a detailed account of the incredible situation in which he found himself. One can imagine the amazement of the man ! And contrary to all expectations, the prosecutor took an extraordinary decision: no doubt moved by such an unwavering desire to defend his country, he did not condemned René, but on the contrary handed him over to the British authorities who finally accepted him, officially. So it was finally as an Englishman that René, the young Norman boy, set out towards his destiny.

This story is incredible, and yet it is absolutely true: the facts were reported in the local press of the time, where I discovered them in the archives. This affair, obviously, raises many questions: and in particular, how is it possible that the British military authorities allowed a young Frenchman who spoke only three words of English to wear their uniform, to join their army and being entrusted with responsibilities without any supporting documents or official papers ? Without being part of any defined batallion? It's strange. We also don't really know what happened next, what his journey was, which front he was sent to, and if he survived. Was he slaughtered in his youth, wading through a filthy mud mixed with blood, coming out of a trench, like hundreds of thousands of others? On the contrary, did he manage to survive the massacre and return to his Normandy to live his life there and - who knows? - find happiness there? So, it's true, a lot of pieces are missing in our puzzle, but the adventure of this teen boy viscerally convinced to make the right choice is further proof that History is a complex and fascinating tapestry made of modest personal stories, deeply human, beyond the great statesmen, the great feats of arms and the complexities of politics.

René, thanks to his determination and also perhaps a little with the unconsciousness of his age, had finally achieved his goal: to participate actively in this terrible conflict, this atrocious war that everybody believed to be the last.

A cold, sad mist floats over the graves of the young men who fell in the war.

A MAN THOUGHT TO BE DEAD COMES BACK TO LIFE IN FECAMP

In the nineteenth century, and particularly during the Victorian period, the British press was full of thrilling stories. Readers were extremely keen to read these news, especially if they were particularly bizarre or gory. National or regional newspapers carried local news, of course, or news that concerned the nation as a whole, but international news also featured prominently in the columns. This was not surprising: under Queen Victoria's reign, Britain was the most powerful country not only in Europe but in the world, and its economic, political and cultural influence extended almost to the four corners of the earth. The Morning Post was a rather conservative London daily newspaper, founded in 1772, which distinguished itself from its competitors by its strong focus on foreign affairs, especially from 1876 onwards. It sent correspondents to every continent to report on the field. The Morning Post was even the first English newspaper to send a woman war reporter, in 1881, to cover the terrible events of the Boer conflict in South Africa. She was Lady Florence Dixie, a colourful, no-nonsense character. In 1937 the Morning Post merged with the Daily Telegraph, which of course can still be found today.

In its issue of 2 November 1896, the Morning Post published an account of a curious affair that took place in Normandy, in the charming and busy port of Fécamp. Here are the facts: today, the Valmont road is a modern road, which allows you to get to the port of Fécamp in a few minutes from the lovely village of Valmont, dominated by its castle. Or the other way round, naturally. But in the past, it was not like that. To get to Valmont, you had to walk along muddy paths with countless ruts. The carts struggled to make headway on this hazardous route. Fortunately, the municipal council of Fécamp, during its meeting of 2 January 1834, decided to put an end to these inconveniences, which made everyone unhappy, and to finally build a road worthy of the name, which would link Fécamp to Yvetot, while passing through Valmont. Well, the inhabitants were still obliged to wait a few more years in the ruts and stones of the road, in fact until the actual start of work in May 1839, because the expropriation of the land had dragged on. By 1896, the date of the story in the Morning Post, the road was completed. And it was there that passers-by found the body of a man lying on the ground one morning. They approached him, knelt down to help him, looked at him: no doubt, it was too late, he was dead.

The man had obviously died suddenly of natural causes, and was immediately recognised as old Godefroy, a neighbour in his eighties, who did not come home every day. Ah, good old Godefroy! Never late for a good glass of Calvados strong liquor! The funeral took place very quickly. Two of the man's daughters were present at the ceremony, and even though their eyes had been heavily misted with tears, they had indeed recognised their father's corpse. When the body was laid to rest and the procession dispersed, the two daughters returned home with a sigh. But when they opened the door of their house... old Godefroy was there, sitting in his usual place in front of the fireplace !

Terrorized, the two women screamed and stood still, while the old man, whom they were sure was a ghost, a spirit returning from the dead, slowly turned his head and stared at them in astonishment! All this commotion obviously alerted the inhabitants of the surrounding houses, who rushed into the dwelling from which the horrible screams were coming, and they too remained speechless before this hallucinating spectacle.

The women lost consciousness, they had to be assisted, they had to be made to recover their senses, people were busy, they were jostling each other, they were agitated, in a hurry. The confusion was total... And in the meantime, the so-called ghost had risen and was approaching! In the first few seconds, people recoiled in fright, they made signs of the cross, someone shouted that they should call the priest immediately.

But almost suddenly it became clear that he was... as alive as you and I !

The key to the mystery? The Morning Post journalist gave the answer: The man buried was an unknown fellow, but his resemblance to the old Godefroy was so extraordinary that no one, not even his own daughters, had been able to notice anything. In the end, this true story, whose echo had crossed the Channel, ended in joy, songs... and a few good bottles of cider !

The abbey of the Holy Trinity, in Fécamp.

SKELETONS PILED UP UNDER THE ROOF

The coronavirus pandemic that the whole world has suffered has taken its toll everywhere. Tens of thousands of people have died. Who could have imagined this a few months earlier? And when you see what has happened in many other countries around the world, you have to wonder. In fact, nothing, absolutely nothing and no one could have predicted what the future would be like. If the overly catastrophic speeches were useless, the overly optimistic positions, as if all this were already behind us once and for all, are basically just a variant of the Coué method : it suffices to repeat that one is well in order to be well ! Faced with a perfectly natural but totally new phenomenon, there is no ready-made answer. Of course, the health systems we have today in the XXIst century are nothing like those available in previous centuries, which is to say not much, but still, This famous Covid 19 that took everyone by surprise demonstrates the fact that our contemporary Western societies have forgotten how much our ancestors had accepted the permanent health risk, how the fear of epidemics was rightly part of their lives, just as the terrible infant mortality or famines due to poor harvests were part of their lives. At any moment, the drama could begin again. No one was safe, no matter what their age or social status.

Let's take the example of the most famous epidemic, the plague. Immediately, one thinks of the great plague of 1348 / 1350, the so-called Black Death. It arrived in Rouen in July 1348, then spread to Caen in October, and to Coutances in November of the same year. And very quickly, the whole region was affected, except perhaps for a few very isolated country parishes, with a frightening mortality rate. The terrible disease reached the shores of England in June 1348, arriving in London in September. On both sides of the Channel, there was no cure for the epidemic except luck, prayer or flight, and its inexorable advance terrorised the entire population and became deeply embedded in the collective consciousness. This mysterious evil was seen as an instrument of divine wrath, and there were countless candles lit and processions held in an attempt to appease it, obviously without much success. Black flags were hoisted on church steeples, people drank the fiery words of preachers predicting the end of the world, large fires were lit on street corners in the hope of clearing the atmosphere, people lost their minds and ran aimlessly screaming, People shut themselves up in their homes, with all doors and windows closed, carts overflowing with corpses roamed the streets in a frightening procession, the brotherhoods of Charitons brought help to the dying as best they could, the apocalypse was near.

If the great Black Death of the Middle Ages has terribly marked the collective imagination by its suddenness and virulence, it was by no means the last in Normandy. Unfortunately, when we consult the archives, we are amazed to discover epidemic outbreaks that have continually resurfaced over the centuries. The plague returned to Rouen for two years, in 1521 and 1522. In Argentan, it raged in 1554, 1558, and 1597. In Harfleur and the surrounding area, it claimed many victims for six years in a row, from 1609 to 1615. In 1619, it moved to Bayeux, Caen and Vire. From 1619 to 1624, it was in Gisors, Louviers and Dieppe. In 1622, it was Tinchebray, in the Orne department, which was hit. Then in 1625, it struck in Coutances and throughout the Cotentin region. For six years, from 1633 to 1639, it returned to Alençon, Argentan and Domfront. The list goes on and on, practically until the XVIIIth century. In these troubled times, one of the most popular saints has always been Saint Roch. This character was born in Montpellier at the end of the XIIIth century, and travelled to Italy, where the plague was already raging in Tuscany. Seeing the sick, he offered to cure them, and the disease miraculously disappeared from the city. Nevertheless, he was himself infected on his return to France. Taking refuge in a forest, he met a dog who brought him bread, became his companion and contributed to his recovery, which was also miraculous. After many adventures, he died at the age of thirty, and legend has it that a message was found on his body saying: *"Those who are struck by the plague and implore the favour of Saint Roch will be cured"*. Several Norman churches still have statues of Saint Roch, and there is a particularly nice local ceremony around this tradition: it is still held today in August in the tiny village of Reux, which is in the Calvados region of the Auge, not far from Pont-L'évêque. In honour of Saint Roch, dog owners can come and have their dogs blessed by the priest in the church square, which dates from the end of the 15th century, after a special mass. A similar ceremony also takes place in Pont d'Ouilly, in the Orne department. The village lies on the pilgrimage route from Rouen to Mont Saint Michel. The blessing of the dogs is preceded by a procession during which the solid wooden statue of the saint is carried through the surrounding fields. This is called the Grand Pardon de Saint Roch, and the chapel of the same name was built in the XVIth century and extensively restored in the early 1930s. Today, large frescoes, covering seventy square meters, depicting the life of the saint can be seen, an original creation by the painter Maurice Le Scouezec.

And what about architecture? Well, Normandy today possesses at least two major, and extremely rare, witnesses to these dreadful times. The first is in Montivilliers, just outside Le Havre: the Aître Brisgaret. This site was built in the XVIth century, from 1542 onwards, to house the bodies of the countless plague victims, as the cemetery in the town centre had become far too small. The corpses were first buried in a mass grave and then, as nature took its course, the bones were collected and piled up under the roof, which thus served as an ossuary. The building consists of a large gallery supported by wooden pillars. These pillars are all remarkably well carved and well preserved, and these spectacular images are particularly representative of the fears of the time. There are two main themes: firstly, the undead in the form of frightening skeletons brandishing scythes or other instruments, symbolising the fragility of earthly existence. Secondly, religious emblems and objects recalling the Passion of the Christ, which can evoke faith in holy eternity. The second major Norman site is located in the very heart of Rouen : the Aître Saint-Maclou. The origin of the Aître Saint Maclou dates back to 1362. As in

Montivilliers, it is a gallery organised around a quadrangle, with the same functions: deposit of corpses in a central cemetery, then storage of the bones on the upper floor. The stone columns are decorated with fine sculptures, some of which were unfortunately damaged during the Wars of Religion, while the beams are adorned with extraordinary carvings representing skulls, tibias, and the tools of the gravediggers. And let's not forget a sad and awful detail: in a niche is a mummified cat. This unfortunate animal has probably been walled up alive in order to chase away the spirit of the Devil. It's enough to make you shiver !

Sculpture of the Aître Saint Maclou, Rouen.

Religious ceremonies are still performed in honor of Saint Roch, the patron saint against the plague.

EPILOGUE

Those who think that devoting oneself to historical and heritage research is to travel through a frozen universe are mistaken. On the contrary, if these explorations through time are exhilarating, it is precisely because they are constantly marked by surprise, questioning and doubt. History is perpetually young because it is always in motion, and new discoveries can call into question supposedly immutable facts. Perpetually young too, thanks to the diversity and multiplicity of encounters with these characters of the past who often resemble us so much.

Let us continue our investigations: the adventure has only just begun.

Welcome to Normandy!

The magnificent cathedral of Rouen

Detail of Rouen cathedral

Many thanks to those in charge of archives, librarians, museum curators, architects and all heritage professionals, in France and England, who have placed their trust in me and allowed me to pursue my research for so many years.